When PANDA feels SMALL

First published in 2025 by North Parade Publishing
Copyright © North Parade Publishing
All rights reserved.

North Parade Publishing Ltd
3-6 Henrietta Mews,
Bath UK
BA2 6LR

www.nppbooks.co.uk

This edition is printed in 2025 exclusively for
WS Pacific Publications, Inc.
Manila, Philippines
www.learningisfun.com.ph

ISBN 978-1-183509-429-7

Printed and bound in China.

When PANDA feels SMALL

Gemma Cary
Krishna Kumar

Far away from here, in a forest of bamboo,
a panda and her grandmother come **strolling** into view.
"How was school today, my dear?" Grandma asks the cub.
The little panda **pauses**, thinks, and gives her head a **rub**.

Quietly she says, "I suppose it was okay, but I don't think I did very **well** at anything today."

Later that evening, when little Panda's gone to bed,
a great idea **pops** into Grandma Panda's head.

Then at the weekend, sleepy little Panda wakes to see some **tickets** in the kitchen. "What are these? Are they for me?" Grandma smiles **broadly** at her. "No, they're for US. Two tickets for a football match and two more for the bus!"

Panda LOVES a football match. She has a favorite team. Just putting on their red scarf is enough to make her **beam**.

She **chatters** on their journey, starts **singing** on the bus…

…and when they have to queue up, Panda doesn't make a fuss.

She spots her **favorite** player and gets ever so excited, and when she gets her autograph, she's even **more** delighted!

She's not disappointed when the match ends in a draw.
She **fist bumps** other fans with her furry little paw.

Grandma tells her afterward, "It's **great** to see you smile. Maybe I could take you to the junior team's next trial?" Little Panda shakes her head. "I'm too big and slow." Grandma replies with a smile, "You should have a go."

The following weekend, Panda shows up at the trial. She's trembling. She hasn't felt this **nervous** for a while…

Soon, the others demonstrate their great **skills** with the ball: flicking, dribbling, shooting – they can do it all!
Panda **tries** to keep up, but compared to them, she's slow.
The others do not pass to her. She doesn't get a go.

After, Panda's **frustrated**.
She doesn't want to speak.
"Never mind," the coach says kindly.
"Come along next week."

At next week's session, Panda's teammates practice ball control.
Panda's really **struggling**, so Coach puts her in goal.
As the ball soars nearer to her, Panda tries to **leap**.
The football **hits** the net and Panda ends up in a heap!

"You just need lots of practice, darling," Grandma says that night.

Panda sighs the **longest** sigh. "I wish that you were right. But when I'm on the pitch, no one trusts me with the ball. I'm the **biggest** player, but they make me feel **small**."

At her debut match, Panda watches her team play.
Then Monkey **twists** his ankle.
Coach needs her to save the day.

She **bumbles** all around the pitch, she **fumbles** with the ball, and when her teammates **grumble,** she feels extra-extra-small. At the half-time whistle, Panda's team is two-nil down. Coach gives everyone a **pep talk,** trying not to frown.

Behind the scenes, a certain player catches Grandma's eye. Grandma asks if she would mind just quickly popping by…

Soon the pair are cheering very **loudly** from their seats.
When Panda catches sight of them, some **magic** hits her feet!
Her **confidence** starts growing. Panda cannot help but **smile**.
If Super Sam has come to watch, she'll make it worth
her while!

Soon Panda starts believing that she **belongs** on the team.
Now she's playing better – and it feels like a dream!
She's not the **fastest** player, or **nimble** on her feet,
but if she can **defend** the goal, they might avoid defeat.

She blocks the ball and sends it flying with a **mighty** kick. Her teammate **boots** it in the goal with one ingenious flick!

Panda's celebrating as the ball comes back in play.
She **accidentally** heads it and she sends it on its way.

"GOAL!" her teammates cry out as it **settles** in the net.

The team all **leap** upon her in a hug she won't forget!

She's up and down the pitch, and she is getting tired when, in the **final** minutes, her teammates score again!

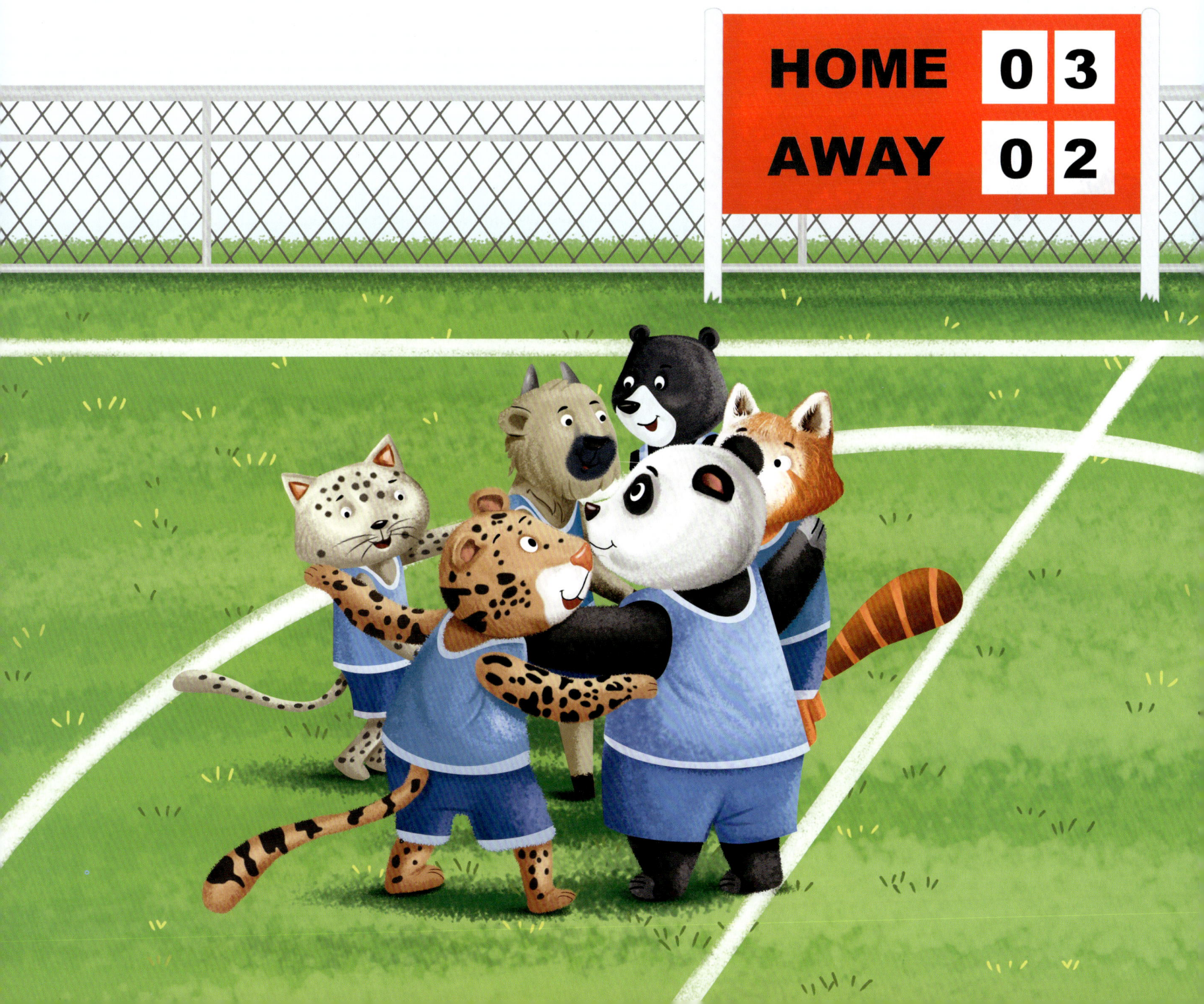

Panda's **greeted** off the pitch by Grandma and the star. "Well done, Panda!" Sam says. "What a **superstar** you are!"

"You see, Panda," whispers Grandma. "We believed in you.
Just have faith and trust yourself and see what you can do!
However **big** you are, you must always **stand up tall,**
and then no one will be able to make you feel small."

NOTES FOR PARENTS

When someone feels small, it might be because they think they're not good enough or clever enough. The best way to boost their self-esteem is to provide love, reassurance, and attention, making sure they know that you're there for them.

TIPS FOR INSPIRING CONFIDENCE IN YOUR CHILD

- If your child seems to have low self-esteem, acknowledge how they are feeling and encourage them to talk about it.

- Model being confident yourself as much as possible, especially in social situations.

- Remind your child that while only one person can be the best at something, everyone can try to achieve their personal best.

- If your child is being left out or ignored by others, try broadening their social horizons, for example by hosting play dates, joining a new club, or trying a new hobby. Then give them lots of praise.

- At bedtime each night, encourage your child to say three good things that happened that day. This will help them to concentrate on the positive things about themselves and others.